Original title:
Reflecting Love

Copyright © 2024 Swan Charm
All rights reserved.

Author: Sara Säde
ISBN HARDBACK: 978-9916-89-022-6
ISBN PAPERBACK: 978-9916-89-023-3
ISBN EBOOK: 978-9916-89-024-0

Nectar of Our Union

In twilight's glow, we find our grace,
Sweet whispers shared in a secret place.
Hearts entangled, forever bound,
In each other's love, comfort is found.

Golden moments flow like wine,
With every heartbeat, you are mine.
Together we dance, joy unconfined,
In the nectar of our union, we unwind.

A Journal of Perceptions

Ink spills thoughts on an empty page,
Each line reveals a new stage.
Through the lens of life, we see,
Perceptions shape our destiny.

Every moment captured bright,
In shadows and in sunlight.
The journal of our hearts we write,
In stories woven, pure delight.

Unspoken Conversations

Eyes meet softly across the room,
In silence blooms a vibrant tune.
Words unsaid, yet understood,
In the depths of hearts, we linger good.

A glance, a smile, a touch of grace,
Unspoken truths in every space.
In quietude, our souls embrace,
An eternal bond, love's gentle trace.

Charmed by Your Presence

Like stars that twinkle in the night,
Your presence fills my world with light.
With every laugh and every sigh,
You cast a spell, and time slips by.

Radiating warmth, so pure and rare,
Moments shared, beyond compare.
Charmed by you, I truly see,
The magic in what we can be.

Enchanted Moments

In twilight's glow, we find our place,
Whispers of dreams in soft embrace.
Stars awaken, one by one,
Magic lingers, day is done.

With every glance, the world stands still,
Time unravels, a sweet thrill.
Moments cherished, hearts aligned,
In this dance, our souls combined.

The Warmth of Your Presence

In shadows cast, your light breaks through,
A gentle touch, so warm and true.
Laughter echoing, hearts alive,
In your presence, I truly thrive.

With every heartbeat, love unfolds,
Stories shared, as life beholds.
Together, facing stormy weather,
In the warmth, we find forever.

Lighthouses in the Dark

Amidst the waves, a beacon shines,
Guiding souls through tangled lines.
In the night, we seek our way,
Lighthouses bright, never sway.

Through raging storms and whispered fears,
Your light remains, calming tears.
In the dark, we hold on tight,
Together, we embrace the night.

The Promise of Tomorrow

As dawn awakes, the sun will rise,
Painting hope across the skies.
With open hearts, we chase the light,
The promise blooms, bold and bright.

Each moment whispers, dreams to weave,
In every breath, the chance believe.
Together we'll journey, hand in hand,
Creating futures, just as planned.

The Art of Being

In silent moments, we find our truth,
A whisper of life, a breath of youth.
Colors of dreams blend and sway,
Creating a canvas for each new day.

Each heartbeat echoes a song of grace,
A journey adorned with time's embrace.
Learning the dance of joy and pain,
In the art of being, wisdom we gain.

Under the Branches of Forever

Beneath the branches, time stands still,
Whispers of breezes, soft and chill.
Leaves like secrets, tangled and bright,
Stories of shadows blended with light.

In the hush of dusk, dreams take flight,
Carried by stars into the night.
The world unfolds in tender embrace,
Under the branches, we find our place.

Sunlit Memories

Golden rays dance on faces aglow,
Woven in laughter, a magical flow.
Moments preserved like sand in a jar,
Each grain a memory, cherished and far.

In the warmth of the sun, we breathe and smile,
Time stretches gently, mile by mile.
With every sunset, stories reframe,
Sunlit memories call out our name.

The Essence We Share

In every glance, a spark ignites,
Threads of connection, woven in lights.
A tapestry rich, with love and care,
The essence we share, beyond compare.

In laughter and tears, we find our way,
Hand in hand, come what may.
Together we blossom, through thick and thin,
In the essence we share, our journey begins.

Raindrop Reveries

Raindrops dance upon the ground,
Whispers of the sky abound.
Nature's tears, a gentle song,
In their rhythm, we belong.

Puddles form like mirrors bright,
Reflecting dreams that take to flight.
Each drop tells a story true,
Of love and loss, of me and you.

The world slows down, a quiet sigh,
As clouds drift softly in the sky.
Underneath their muted grace,
We find our thoughts in a sacred space.

With every splash, a memory wakes,
Reminding us of the paths we take.
In this symphony of rain,
We find joy amidst the pain.

So let it fall, this rain so sweet,
Embrace the rhythm, feel the beat.
In every drop, a chance to start,
Raindrop reveries, close to the heart.

Hues of Harmony

In the garden, colors bloom,
Painting life, dispelling gloom.
Petals whisper soft and low,
Hues of harmony in a row.

Lavender, gold, a sunset's flare,
Each shade tells a tale laid bare.
Brush the canvas, let it flow,
In every stroke, a love we sow.

Nature's palette, rich and vast,
Moments captured, forever last.
Through blossoms bright, we find our way,
In vibrant colors, hearts convey.

Tangled vines and sunlit beams,
Dance along with woven dreams.
Each hue a note in life's sweet song,
Together, we find where we belong.

So let us paint with pure intent,
A symphony of colors spent.
In every shade, our spirits rise,
Hues of harmony beneath the skies.

Beyond the Canvas

A canvas stretched beneath the light,
Holds whispers of dreams, pure and bright.
Brush meets surface, a tale unfolds,
In colors bold, a heart's story told.

With every stroke, emotions flow,
As the artist seeks to let love show.
Imagery born from deep within,
The magic of life, where we begin.

Shadows fall and colors clash,
Moments captured in a flash.
Beyond the canvas, worlds ignite,
Imagination soars, taking flight.

Each creation, a window wide,
Inviting all to step inside.
To venture forth, to feel and see,
Beyond the canvas, we are free.

So let the art of life be shared,
In every heartbeat, souls laid bare.
With open hearts, we find the way,
Beyond the canvas, we will stay.

The Pulse of Connection

In the silence, a heartbeat calls,
Echoing through the crowded halls.
A thread that binds us, soft but strong,
In every whisper, we belong.

Eyes meet eyes, a knowing glance,
In fleeting moments, shared romance.
With every laugh, our spirits blend,
The pulse of connection never ends.

Through life's chaos, we find our tune,
Dancing softly beneath the moon.
Each fleeting touch, a fleeting spark,
Guiding us through the endless dark.

The rhythm of life, with every breath,
Through joy and pain, beyond mere death.
In the tapestry of time we weave,
The pulse of connection, we believe.

So take my hand, we'll journey far,
Through tangled paths, where wonders are.
In every heartbeat, close your eyes,
The pulse of connection never dies.

Two Hearts as One

In the quiet night, we stand,
Two hearts beating, hand in hand.
Whispers soft, a bond so tight,
Together we shine, a guiding light.

With every touch, a spark ignites,
In unison, we scale new heights.
Through storms and calm, we will prevail,
Our love's a ship, we'll never sail.

Moments shared, joy intertwined,
In every smile, our souls aligned.
Time passes, yet we remain,
Two hearts as one, through joy and pain.

No distance great can pull apart,
For love resides within the heart.
In every dream, in every prayer,
Two hearts united, forever rare.

As seasons change, our love will grow,
In gentle winds, our feelings flow.
Together we'll dance, embracing fate,
Two hearts as one, it's never too late.

Sunflower Kisses

In fields of gold, we laugh and play,
Sunflower kisses, brightening the day.
Your smile shines like the sun so high,
Together we reach for the endless sky.

Petals swaying in a warm sweet breeze,
Moments like these, they always please.
With every glance, the world feels right,
Two hearts entwined, such pure delight.

Beneath the blooms, secrets we share,
In every whisper, a tender care.
Nature's beauty in the softest hue,
Sunflower kisses, forever true.

As dusk arrives, the stars will gleam,
In twilight whispers, we weave a dream.
Among the flowers, our spirits soar,
In sunflower fields, we're wanting more.

Through seasons' change, our love will stand,
Like sunflowers reaching for golden land.
Hand in hand, through laughter and tears,
Sunflower kisses, erase our fears.

Beyond the Horizon of Us

We journey forth, hand in hand,
Beyond horizons, where dreams expand.
In unknown lands, our compass true,
With every step, I walk with you.

Through valleys deep and mountains wide,
In every challenge, love is our guide.
Stars above, they light our way,
Together we shine, come what may.

Whispers of hope in the evening air,
A promise kept, a love so rare.
With open hearts beneath the sky,
Beyond the horizon, we will fly.

Days may fade, but we'll remain,
Through stormy skies and gentle rain.
In every heartbeat, a secret trust,
Beyond the horizon, it's just us.

The world may shift, but we are bold,
Sharing stories yet to be told.
Into the sunset, love will beam,
Beyond the horizon, we're living the dream.

An Ode to Togetherness

In every laugh, a music sweet,
An ode to us, where hearts do meet.
With every moment, time will bind,
A tapestry of love combined.

In cozy corners, we find our peace,
Through trials faced, our joys increase.
In quiet sighs and gentle touch,
Together we conquer, it means so much.

With every dawn, our hope renews,
In morning light, we'll find our muse.
Grateful hearts that rise and sing,
An ode to togetherness, love's offering.

Through shifting sands and tides that change,
In every glance, we rearrange.
A bond unbroken, forever we stand,
Together as one, hand in hand.

In every sunset's golden glow,
An echo of love we choose to show.
In this beautiful dance, come what may,
An ode to togetherness, day by day.

Lost in Your Laughter

Your laughter dances in the air,
A melody sweet, free from despair.
It twirls like leaves in autumn's breeze,
Bringing warmth, making moments seize.

Echoes linger where joy's entwined,
In every corner of heart and mind.
A symphony, each giggle shared,
A treasure found, a love declared.

Garden of Shared Dreams

In the garden where wishes bloom,
Every petal dispels the gloom.
With sunlight kissing every leaf,
We nurture hope, banish grief.

Together we plant the seeds of fate,
Watering thoughts, never late.
In the shadows, we laugh and play,
Creating a path, come what may.

Chasing the Dawn Together

As night surrenders to the light,
We rise together, hearts in flight.
Chasing horizons with eager eyes,
Finding the beauty in sunlit skies.

With each step, our dreams take wing,
In whispered hopes, our spirits sing.
With hands entwined, we journey on,
Into the warmth of every dawn.

The Gentle Tide of Us

Like waves that kiss the sandy shore,
Our love ebbs and flows, wanting more.
In the calm, in the stormy testing,
Together we stand, forever resting.

Each moment shared, a ripple wide,
A journey where our hearts abide.
In the vast sea, you're my guide,
Through every tide, you're by my side.

The Dance of Warmth

In the glow of the fading light,
Shadows sway, day bids goodnight.
Whispers of leaves, soft and near,
Nature sings, the heart will cheer.

Feet tread lightly on the ground,
Where memories in steps are found.
Stars unveil their twinkling gleam,
Guiding hearts in the twilight dream.

Embers flicker in the cool air,
A spirit of warmth everywhere.
Together we spin in delight,
Holding close through the starry night.

Moments weave like a gentle tide,
In this space, we shall abide.
The dance of warmth, tender and bright,
Keeps us close, hearts taking flight.

As dawn whispers, shadows retreat,
Our rhythm flows, a heartbeat sweet.
Through every turn, love's embrace,
In this dance, we find our place.

Fragments of Us

Across the sea of endless dreams,
We gather pieces, torn at seams.
In laughter's echo, in silence too,
Fragments of us come shining through.

Moments captured, like grains of sand,
Held in the palm of a caring hand.
Each memory a thread so fine,
Woven together, our hearts align.

Time may stretch, or it may bend,
In every dawn, we find a friend.
Through storm and calm, we rise anew,
These fragments shine, a radiant hue.

In whispered secrets, stories unfold,
From silver moonlight to sunsets bold.
Every laugh shared, every tear cried,
In these fragments, our love abides.

So let us cherish the paths we roam,
Turning fragments into a home.
For in this journey, we trust and see,
Forever, it's you and me.

Radiance in the Quiet

In the hush of the evening glow,
Stillness sings, the world moves slow.
Gentle whispers through leaves sway,
Radiance wraps the winding way.

In shadows deep, light finds its way,
Painting dreams in shades of gray.
Moments linger, soft and clear,
Echoes of peace we hold so dear.

Stars appear, a delicate lace,
In this calm, we find our place.
Hearts attuned to the silent night,
Finding comfort in shared delight.

Every heartbeat, a melody sweet,
In the quiet, our souls meet.
With every breath, we feel the grace,
In tranquil spaces, love we trace.

So let the world drift far away,
In this calm, let us stay and play.
For the radiance in quiet moments,
Is a language of hearts' true components.

Embrace of the Dawn

As the sky blushes into day,
Soft lights chase the night away.
In the cradle of morning's smile,
Hope awakens, free of guile.

Birds take flight with songs to sing,
Welcoming warmth that the day will bring.
Beneath the sun's gentle kiss,
Every moment unfolds in bliss.

With each ray that kisses the ground,
New beginnings in silence found.
Hands entwined, we step outside,
In the embrace of dawn, we glide.

Every breath a fresh start anew,
In this light, our dreams break through.
Together we rise, unafraid to roam,
Wherever the dawn may call us home.

So let us stand as shadows fade,
In the day's glow, let love cascade.
For in the dawn's embrace so warm,
We find our peace, weather any storm.

Paper Cranes in the Breeze

In the sky, they gracefully glide,
Wings unfold, with dreams inside.
Each fold whispers, tales untold,
Carried gently, in the wind's hold.

Colors bright against the blue,
Hopes and wishes born anew.
With each turn, a dance they weave,
A fragile magic, we believe.

Drifting softly, they unite,
Bearing love, a pure delight.
Through the air, their stories soar,
Leaving hearts to crave for more.

Caught in currents, soaring high,
'Til they vanish, in the sky.
Yet their spirit, we embrace,
In each heart, they find a place.

Paper cranes, a fleeting sight,
Symbol of peace, a guiding light.
In their flight, our dreams expand,
Together, we will stand, hand in hand.

Under the Stars' Embrace

Beneath a blanket, dark and deep,
Where ancient secrets softly creep.
Stars like lanterns, brightly burn,
In their glow, we take our turn.

Whispers of the night surround,
In quiet moments, solace found.
Dreams awaken, fears laid bare,
In this haven, love will share.

Laughter mingles with the breeze,
As shadows dance among the trees.
Each twinkle speaks of tales once told,
Of destinies entwined, and bold.

Holding close, we gaze above,
In the vastness, stars we love.
Cocooned within the universe,
Two hearts, joined in a cosmic verse.

Underneath this endless sky,
We find the truth, we learn to fly.
In the light of every star's embrace,
We discover our sacred space.

Silent Echoes of Joy

In the stillness, laughter rings,
Softly echoing, joy it brings.
Every smile, a gentle sound,
In quiet corners, love is found.

Fleeting moments, time stands still,
Every heartbeat, every thrill.
Softest whispers, in the air,
Silent echoes everywhere.

In the shadows, memories gleam,
Woven through a shared dream.
Colors of past, bright and warm,
Against the cold, they serve as balm.

Amidst the silence, hearts will sing,
Summoning warmth, joy takes wing.
Gentle murmurs guide the way,
In this stillness, night and day.

Silent echoes linger on,
In the dawn, until they're gone.
Yet within, they'll ever flow,
In the heart, their light will glow.

When Time Stands Still

In moments trapped within a glance,
Time halts here, a timeless dance.
The world outside fades away,
In this bubble, we shall stay.

Every heartbeat, slow and pure,
In this stillness, we are sure.
Silent promises softly made,
In the quiet, fears allayed.

Every touch, electric spark,
In the shadows, ignites a mark.
Eyes locked tight, we drift away,
Into dreams where memories play.

The clock may tick, but we enthrall,
Caught in moments, we have it all.
Floating gently on this thrill,
A sanctuary, when time stands still.

Forever held in this embrace,
Two souls lost in love's sweet grace.
As dawn breaks, we'll still remain,
In the stillness, joy unfeigned.

Whispers in the Moonlight

In the silver glow of night,
Soft whispers float, taking flight.
Stars above, they lightly gleam,
As I drift into a dream.

Crickets sing their sweet refrain,
Notes of love in gentle pain.
The breeze carries tales untold,
Secrets wrapped in shadows bold.

The moon, a witness to our fate,
Gazes down, whispers innate.
In this realm, where silence reigns,
Love unfurls, like gentle rains.

Every shimmer holds a sigh,
Every glance, a sweet goodbye.
In this moment, hearts align,
Two souls dance, a love divine.

With each breath, the night will pass,
Time dissolves like fragile glass.
Yet, beneath the moon's soft light,
We find peace in endless night.

Echoes of Your Heart

In the quiet of the dawn,
Your heartbeat calls, a sweet song.
Each pulse sends waves through the air,
In this moment, none compare.

Your laughter, like a gentle breeze,
Whispers secrets, sets me at ease.
Within your eyes, reflections dance,
Lost in the depths, in a trance.

The world fades, it's just us two,
Every echo whispers 'I do.'
With every heartbeat, we define,
A love that transcends space and time.

Through shadows deep and valleys low,
We walk together, steady flow.
Each step echoes, synchronizing,
A rhythm found, so mesmerizing.

With every heartbeat, love does grow,
In every moment, let it show.
For in this life, let it be known,
Your heart, my home, we are not alone.

Mirror of Our Souls

In your eyes, I see my truth,
Reflections of our fleeting youth.
Every glance reveals the flame,
A spirit wild, yet untamed.

With every word, a symphony,
Harmonies of you and me.
In silence, our hearts entwine,
A melody, sweet and divine.

Each laugh is a spark, a light,
Illuminating the darkest night.
In your smile, I find my way,
A guide through shadows and dismay.

As the world spins ever fast,
I hold on to moments that last.
Our whispers weave a tapestry,
Of love that flows endlessly.

Together, we craft a whole,
You are the mirror to my soul.
In the depths, where love unfurls,
We find our place in this vast world.

Threads of Togetherness

Interwoven hearts collide,
In every moment, side by side.
Threads of fate that gently bind,
Two souls dancing, intertwined.

Every laugh, a vibrant hue,
Paints our canvas bold and true.
In the tapestry of our days,
Each thread tells of love's pure ways.

Through storms that shake and winds that wail,
Together, we will always sail.
With hands held tight against the fray,
We journey on, come what may.

A quilt of memories we create,
Sewn with patience, never late.
Each stitch a promise, firm and tight,
Through every shadow, we find light.

As seasons shift and years unfold,
Our love grows richer, more than gold.
For in this life, come joy, come strife,
Together, we embrace this life.

A Symphony of Emotions

In whispers soft, the heartbeats play,
Melodies of joy that gently sway.
A sorrowful note, a laughter's spark,
Each feeling dances, lighting the dark.

With every crescendo, the spirit flies,
Yet in the silence, a lullaby sighs.
The crescendo builds, then fades away,
A symphony born in the light of day.

Shadows and sunlight, they intertwine,
Every sweet moment, a taste of divine.
Harmony's touch, both tender and bold,
In every echo, a story unfolds.

Within our souls, the music thrives,
Breathing life into our everyday lives.
Each chord a memory, a promise to keep,
In the symphony's arms, dreams softly sleep.

So let us listen, with hearts open wide,
To the song of emotions, a vibrant tide.
For in this orchestra, we all belong,
Together we thrive, together we're strong.

Dreams Draped in Moonlight

Under the stars, the night unfolds,
Whispers of dreams that are softly told.
Moonlight bathes the world in a glow,
Guiding our hearts where wanderlust flows.

A silver veil drapes the sleeping land,
Inviting us to dream, to take a stand.
Each twinkling light, a wish in the dark,
Awakens the soul, ignites a spark.

In shadows deep, our fantasies play,
Through ethereal paths where starlights stray.
With every breath, we linger and sway,
In moonlit reveries, we find our way.

The night is young, the universe wide,
With every heartbeat, the dreams collide.
In this tranquil space, let passions ignite,
As dreams drape us softly in the night.

So close your eyes, let your spirit soar,
In the arms of the moon, we are forevermore.
Each moment cherished, a treasure divine,
In dreams draped in moonlight, our souls entwine.

Fleeting Glances

A look exchanged, a moment brief,
In fleeting glances, lies our belief.
Eyes that meet in the crowded space,
Speak silent words that time can't erase.

A fleeting smile, a spark ignites,
A tender brush in the soft twilight.
In those quick seconds, worlds collide,
Two souls dancing on the same tide.

Like whispers carried on the breeze,
Such precious moments bring us to ease.
Each stolen glance a story told,
Of hearts that crave, of dreams that unfold.

In crowded rooms, connections gleam,
A flicker of hope, a shared dream.
Though time may pass, we'll always know,
In fleeting glances, love starts to grow.

So cherish those looks, both bright and shy,
For in their magic, our spirits fly.
Each fleeting moment, a gem to keep,
A glimpse of forever, within the deep.

A Palette of Feelings

A canvas bright with colors bold,
Each hue a story waiting to be told.
Brush strokes of laughter, swirls of pain,
An artwork of life, joy mixed with rain.

Blues of sorrow, greens of peace,
Each shade resonates, never cease.
Crimson passion splattered with flair,
Every emotion found hanging in air.

Golds of hope shimmer, radiate light,
While shadows of doubt play hide-and-seek at night.
A touch of beige for the calm in the storm,
Creating a picture that feels truly warm.

With every layer, we blend and we fight,
Crafting our lives with love shining bright.
A palette of feelings, unique and true,
A masterpiece woven with shades of you.

So let us paint, with hearts open wide,
Each stroke a memory, no need to hide.
In this vast gallery where we all belong,
Together we forge our beautiful song.

Underneath the Starry Veil

Beneath the glow of silver light,
Whispers of dreams take their flight.
Stars twinkle like eyes up high,
Painting night's canvas in the sky.

Cool breezes rustle golden leaves,
Nature's magic, the heart believes.
In shadows dance, two souls entwined,
Love's sweet secret, softly defined.

Moonbeams wrap around our gaze,
Enchanted in this timeless haze.
Every sparkle writes a song,
Where in silence, we both belong.

A tapestry of hope and fears,
Woven gently through the years.
Underneath this starry dome,
We find our place, we find our home.

A Canvas of Emotions

Brush strokes of laughter, shades of tears,
Life unfolds across the years.
Colors blend in joy and strife,
Painting the journey that is life.

Moments captured, vibrant and pure,
Each hue expresses what we endure.
A palette rich with tales untold,
In every brush, a memory bold.

Warm sunlight, soft shadows play,
Dancing emotions in bright array.
In the chaos, we find our grace,
On this canvas, we leave our trace.

From dark to light, we shift and sway,
Creating beauty, come what may.
A masterpiece formed with every choice,
In colors deep, we find our voice.

The Warmth of Shared Moments

Hands held gently in quiet embrace,
Together we find our sacred space.
Laughter lingers, a melody sweet,
In shared moments, our hearts meet.

Sunrise whispers, a brand new day,
In your eyes, I find my way.
Simple joys and whispered sighs,
In your warmth, my spirit flies.

The clock ticks softly, time stands still,
Filling our hearts with a tender thrill.
Every glance, a story spun,
In this haven, we are one.

Life's tapestry woven with care,
Each thread a memory we share.
In love's embrace, as we both know,
The warmth of moments helps us grow.

Whirlwinds of Tenderness

In the eye of the storm, we find our peace,
Amidst the chaos, love will never cease.
Tangled together, we ride the wave,
In whirlwinds of tenderness, we are brave.

Softest breezes caress our skin,
Whispers of truth, where dreams begin.
With every challenge, we stand tall,
Together we rise, we will not fall.

Hearts racing fast, like leaves in flight,
Guided by stars, we chase the light.
In each gust, a promise we make,
Love's gentle strength a bond we stake.

Through every storm, we'll navigate,
In whirlwinds of love, we celebrate.
Each moment precious, a dance divine,
In the rhythm of hearts, forever we shine.

A Voyage in a Teacup

In a teacup small and round,
Whispers of the sea abound.
Sailing waves of fragrant tea,
Charting dreams for you and me.

A gentle breeze begins to sway,
As colors blend in soft ballet.
Steaming stories, rich and bright,
Adventures brewed in morning light.

With each sip, the world unfurls,
Magic dances, twirls and swirls.
We travel far on porcelain seas,
Finding solace in the breeze.

In every drop, a journey told,
Of distant lands and treasures bold.
A teacup holds our dreams, so grand,
A voyage crafted, hand in hand.

So here we sail, just you and I,
Through steaming mists beneath the sky.
In this vessel, time stands still,
A teacup journey, pure and real.

Sunkissed Memories

In the warmth of golden rays,
Laughter lingers, bright and gay.
Moments wrapped in sunlight's glow,
A tapestry of memories flow.

Footprints trace the sandy shore,
Echoes of the days before.
Each shell holds a whispered tale,
As our hopes set forth to sail.

Underneath the azure sky,
Time stands still as breezes sigh.
With every wave, I'm taken back,
To sunlit paths we used to track.

The scent of salt and blooming flowers,
Paints our hearts in fleeting hours.
Sunkissed dreams, a vibrant dance,
Remind us of that sweet romance.

So let us gather these bright days,
And cherish them in countless ways.
For memories, like rays of sun,
Keep our spirits intertwined as one.

Tales of Two Souls

In a world where shadows play,
Two souls find their perfect way.
Hand in hand, they weave a dream,
A tapestry of love's sweet theme.

With every glance, a story starts,
Whispers shared from hearts to hearts.
In quiet moments, magic grows,
As time in tender silence flows.

Stars bear witness to their plight,
Guiding paths through endless night.
Their laughter dances on the breeze,
A lullaby that puts the heart at ease.

Through hills and valleys, they will roam,
Together, they create a home.
No distance can their bond erase,
For every mile, love finds its place.

So let the tales of two souls sing,
Of endless joy that love can bring.
In every heartbeat, stories play,
Forever cherished, come what may.

An Arc of Affection

Beneath the sky, where colors blend,
Two hearts chart paths that never end.
An arc of love that bends and sways,
In every moment, it stays and plays.

With soft smiles and gentle sighs,
They dance together 'neath the skies.
In the hush of evening's glow,
Affection blooms, a gentle flow.

Time cradles their whispered dreams,
In the quiet, love always beams.
Holding hands, they build their fate,
An arc of warmth, a bond so great.

Through all the storms and sunny days,
Their spirits twine in countless ways.
A rainbow arches in their view,
Forever bright, forever true.

So let the world around them spin,
For in their hearts, new journeys begin.
An arc of affection, strong and wide,
Together they stand, side by side.

The Symphony of Silence

In the hush of night, whispers play,
Where shadows linger, dreams softly sway.
Each heartbeat echoes, soft and clear,
A symphony of silence, all we hold dear.

Stars twinkle gently, lighting the dark,
Their flickering glimmers, a guiding spark.
Beneath the vast expanse, we find our peace,
A moment of stillness, where worries cease.

In the cool embrace of the nighttime air,
Thoughts drift like leaves, free from despair.
The world feels lighter, time stands still,
In this tranquil realm, we chase our will.

Voices grow softer, as night descends,
The heart knows its secrets, the silence lends.
With every pause, we breathe it in,
In the symphony of stillness, new dreams begin.

Dances of Starlight

Beneath the heavens, the starlight sways,
In cosmic rhythms, it twirls and plays.
Galaxies twinkle, a radiant dance,
Inviting our souls to join in the trance.

The night sky sparkles, a canvas of dreams,
Whispers of magic flow in moonbeams.
Each star a dancer, with stories to tell,
In the grand performance, we're under their spell.

Winds carry tunes of celestial song,
In this swirling ballet, we all belong.
With every twinkle, hearts synchronize,
Finding the rhythm that never denies.

Together we move, in light's gentle glow,
Through the cosmic waltz, our spirits flow.
In the dance of starlight, we lose all strife,
As the universe celebrates this precious life.

Moments Woven in Time

Threads of memory weave through our days,
In delicate patterns, in myriad ways.
Each moment a stitch in the fabric we share,
Binding us softly, with love and care.

Golden sunrises paint the morning sky,
We grasp fleeting seconds as they drift by.
In laughter and sorrow, in joy and in pain,
The moments we cherish, forever remain.

Beneath the old oak, we carved our dreams,
With whispers of hope flowing like streams.
Time like a river will carry us on,
But the essence of love will never be gone.

As seasons will change and years will unfold,
The stories we cherish will never grow old.
In the tapestry woven, our hearts still align,
In this dance of existence, each thread divine.

Whispers in the Moonlight

Under the moon's glow, secrets reside,
In shadows and light, where dreams can hide.
Whispers of night paint the world anew,
In silvery tones, all thoughts come to view.

The breeze carries tales from ages long past,
A melody sweet, forever to last.
With every soft rustle, the trees as our friends,
They hold our confessions, where silence transcends.

In the glow of the night, time slows its race,
Finding connection in this sacred space.
Hearts speak in murmurs, as stars gently gleam,
In whispers of moonlight, we weave our dream.

With each fleeting moment, souls intertwine,
In a dance of shadows, your heart next to mine.
Let the world fade away, just us in this light,
Lost in sweet whispers, embracing the night.

The Energy Between

In silence shared, a spark ignites,
A glance exchanged, as day turns night.
Electric vibes that flow and swirl,
Two hearts entwined in a lively whirl.

Unseen currents dance with glee,
In every breath, you're close to me.
A rhythm flows, a whispered song,
In this connection, we both belong.

Moments linger, the world fades out,
In this essence, there's no doubt.
A bond unspoken, yet profound,
In this energy, love is found.

Through laughter bright and shadows deep,
In this warmth, our souls do leap.
Together strong, together free,
In the energy between you and me.

Wrapped in Warmth

A cozy fire crackles near,
With every flame, I feel you here.
Wrapped in blankets, soft and tight,
In this embrace, the world feels right.

Your laughter dances with the light,
In this moment, joy takes flight.
The world outside, a distant call,
In your warmth, I have it all.

Fingers intertwined, a gentle squeeze,
With every heartbeat, my spirit's ease.
Soft whispers float in evening air,
In your arms, I find my care.

As seasons change, and shadows grow,
In this haven, love will flow.
Wrapped in warmth, we face the storm,
Together strong, always warm.

The Ballet of Togetherness

In silence shared, we sway and glide,
An elegant dance, side by side.
Each step we take, a perfect rhyme,
In the ballet, love we find.

Twists and turns, a graceful flow,
Two souls entwined, forever glow.
With every leap, our spirits soar,
In this dance, we crave for more.

The world fades as we spin and twirl,
Lost in rhythm, just you and Pearl.
United hearts in perfect time,
In our ballet, love's sublime.

The music plays, our hearts compose,
In this moment, pure love grows.
Forever dancing, you and me,
In the ballet of togetherness, we're free.

Threads of Fate

In the tapestry of time we weave,
Threads of fate that we believe.
A needle's touch, a gentle pull,
In this design, our hearts are full.

Colors bright, and shadows long,
In every stitch, a love song.
Bound together through joy and pain,
In every tear, there's love to gain.

Moments linger, our paths align,
In this fabric, you are mine.
Patterns formed, both strong and free,
In the threads of fate, we simply be.

When storms arise, we hold on tight,
In unity, we find our light.
Through every weave, our story flows,
In the threads of fate, love knows.

Moments Caught in Time

In the stillness of the dawn,
A gentle breeze starts to play,
Whispers of yesterday linger,
As shadows softly fade away.

The laughter of children dances,
In fields where wildflowers sway,
Each smile a fleeting moment,
Captured as clouds drift gray.

Fleeting glances that we treasure,
Sparkle like stars in the night,
Every heartbeat a reminder,
Of love bathed in golden light.

Time weaves stories through our fingers,
With threads of silk and sorrow,
In the tapestry of living,
We'll find a brighter tomorrow.

Moments caught like fireflies,
Glow softly in our minds,
A treasure trove of memory,
In the heart where love aligns.

The Softest Echo

In the twilight's gentle glow,
Whispers dance upon the breeze,
The softest echo of your love,
Brings my restless heart at ease.

Moonbeams spill on whispered dreams,
As silver shadows start to weave,
Each sigh a tale unspoken,
A promise that we both believe.

Through the silence of the night,
Your laughter lingers long,
In every note of starlit song,
I find where I belong.

The echoes of our sweet refrain,
Chase the dark away,
With each heartbeat that I feel,
It's you who lights my way.

Underneath the velvet sky,
I hear the softest song,
Your love a gentle echo,
In my heart where it's so strong.

Heartbeats and Whispers

In the quiet of the evening,
Our heartbeats softly combine,
Each whisper a fragile secret,
That flows like vintage wine.

Hands entwined, we wander,
Through gardens lush and fair,
Every glance a sweet caress,
A promise wrapped in air.

I find solace in your laughter,
Like music in a breeze,
In the garden of our friendship,
I discover all my peace.

With every heartbeat shared in silence,
Time gently slips away,
Within your eyes, I see forever,
Where love decides to stay.

So let the world keep turning,
We'll embrace the sun and rain,
In heartbeats and in whispers,
Together, we remain.

A Tapestry of Us

In every thread of our story,
Colors bleed and blend so bright,
A tapestry of laughter,
Weaving day into night.

From the fabric of our memories,
To the stitches of our dreams,
Together we'll create a world,
Where love flows like gentle streams.

Each moment stitched with kindness,
A pattern rich and bold,
In the loom of life, we gather,
A bond that won't grow old.

Through storms that try to unravel,
We stand firm, side by side,
In the tapestry of our journey,
Our hearts forever tied.

As threads of gold and silver,
Entwine both yours and mine,
In this woven piece of heaven,
I find my heart's design.

Enveloped in Grace

In the quiet of dawn's embrace,
Whispers of peace fill the space.
Gentle breezes softly dance,
Life unfolds in a sweet trance.

Soft petals drop from fragrant blooms,
As sunlight breaks through morning's glooms.
Every shadow, a story told,
In every heart, a spark of gold.

Time skims on with feathered feet,
In moments lost, our dreams repeat.
Cradled in warmth, we find our way,
In every night, a brand new day.

The world spins on in serene light,
Guided by stars through darkest night.
Grace wraps around like a gentle sigh,
In love's pure arms, we learn to fly.

With every heartbeat, hope will rise,
In the soft glow of endless skies.
Embraced by wonders yet unseen,
Our lives a tapestry, woven clean.

Stories Woven in Time

Leaves of ages whisper low,
Tales of past where rivers flow.
Echoes linger in the breeze,
Memories dance among the trees.

Each line penned with love's embrace,
Marks of laughter, loss, and grace.
In the silence, voices speak,
Telling secrets, bold yet weak.

Moments captured, softly spun,
Threads of light 'neath setting sun.
Lives entwined in fate's great loom,
In every heart, a space to bloom.

Through the ages, stories stay,
Guiding lost souls on their way.
Each chapter holds a cherished thrill,
Pages turning with iron will.

From dawn to dusk, our tales entwine,
Bringing forth what's yours and mine.
In every word, a glimpse of home,
In every heart, we're free to roam.

The Chime of Hearts

In echoes soft, love's whispers play,
Chiming softly, come what may.
A melody, sweet yet clear,
Brings forth joy, erases fear.

Bells of hope ring through the night,
Guiding souls toward the light.
Every heartbeat, a song to sing,
In every moment, warmth they bring.

Lingering notes that softly swell,
In each heart, a secret well.
Harmony in every glance,
Love's sweet dance, a sacred chance.

Through valleys deep and mountains high,
Together we rise, together we sigh.
Every chime a bond so true,
In this life, it's me and you.

As stars align and wishes soar,
The chime of hearts forevermore.
With every ring, our spirits soar,
United in love, we fear no more.

Starry-Eyed Confessions

Under the vast and twinkling sky,
Dreams take flight, they drift and fly.
Whispers float on starlit beams,
Carrying the weight of dreams.

With every glance, a truth revealed,
In open hearts, our fates are sealed.
Painting wishes upon the night,
Confessions glow in soft twilight.

Silent vows in shadows cast,
Promises made that forever last.
In the darkness, we find our way,
Guided by the stars' ballet.

Each heartbeat a wish upon the air,
In quiet moments, love lays bare.
With every twinkling, secrets share,
Stars above and dreams to spare.

Every sparkle, a story spun,
As night unfolds, our journey's begun.
Starry-eyed, we chase the light,
In endless love, we find our flight.

Gentle Currents of Emotion

Waves of whispers softly flow,
Tides of feelings, ebb and glow.
Carried by the winds of time,
Hearts entwined in gentle rhyme.

In the stillness, secrets blend,
Silent hopes that gently mend.
As shadows play in fading light,
We drift together, hearts take flight.

Ripples dance on quiet streams,
Flowing softly like our dreams.
Every glance a quiet song,
In this place where we belong.

With the moonlight, we confide,
In these currents, we abide.
Every touch, a soothing balm,
In this moment, we are calm.

Time slows down as we embrace,
In this dance, we find our space.
Gentle currents of the heart,
Binding us, we'll never part.

The Language of Touch

Fingers trace a silent line,
The warmth of skin, a spark divine.
In the stillness, words are few,
Emotions speak, connecting true.

A gentle brush sends shivers deep,
Promises made that we will keep.
In every caress, a story told,
A bond that's treasured, pure as gold.

Across the distance, souls will reach,
In subtle gestures, love's true speech.
A lingering touch, a soft embrace,
Time stands still in this safe space.

Each heartbeat echoes the unspoken,
In this dance, hearts are woven.
Every caress ignites the night,
In the language of touch, pure delight.

Life unfolds in tender grace,
With each moment we can trace.
Through the silence, we find our way,
In the language of touch, we stay.

Crimson Petals and Silver Dews

Beneath the moon, the petals sway,
Crimson dreams of night and day.
Silver dews like diamonds shine,
Nature's beauty, pure, divine.

Whispers carried on the breeze,
In this moment, hearts find ease.
With every bloom, a tale unfolds,
Of love and warmth, of dreams retold.

Raindrops kiss the earth so sweet,
Bringing life beneath our feet.
In the garden, secrets bloom,
Stirring joy, dispelling gloom.

Crimson petals, soft and rare,
Holding wishes in the air.
Silver dews like tears align,
A perfect dance, a love divine.

Under stars, we stand in awe,
Embracing nature's quiet law.
Life's tender beauty we pursue,
In the petals and the dews.

A Dance in Twilight

As day surrenders to the night,
In twilight's glow, our spirits take flight.
Underneath the painted skies,
We find our song where silence lies.

Steps are gentle, hearts aligned,
In this rhythm, love is blind.
With every turn, a spark ignites,
In shadows deep, our souls unite.

Flickering stars begin to shine,
A cosmic dance, a love divine.
With every twirl, we find our place,
Lost in time, in soft embrace.

As night unfolds its velvet hue,
Each whispered dream feels fresh and new.
In the twilight, we are free,
A dance for just you and me.

In this liminal space we sway,
Merging shadows, night and day.
A dance in twilight, so profound,
In love's embrace, we're truly found.

Heartstrings Intertwined

In the silence, whispers blend,
Where two souls begin to mend.
Every glance, a story told,
In this bond, our hearts unfold.

Through the storms, we stand as one,
Chasing dreams beneath the sun.
With every laugh, with every tear,
We find strength, we find each other near.

In the dance of fate, we sway,
Tracing paths that light our way.
Threads of love, a tapestry,
Woven deep in you and me.

With every heartbeat, a vow made,
In shadowed nights, we won't fade.
Together, we rise and shine,
In this journey, love's design.

Hand in hand, we face the light,
In the dark, we hold each tight.
With every moment, time aligns,
In our hearts, the love defines.

The Song of Us

In melodies soft, we entwine,
Harmonies sweet, your heart is mine.
Every note, a memory spun,
In the rhythm, we become one.

With laughter like music, we play,
Catching dreams that float our way.
Through the verses of life we sing,
In every chord, our spirits spring.

In the quiet, our voices rise,
Echoing love beneath the skies.
With each breath, a lyric flows,
In the silence, our essence glows.

As the seasons weave their tune,
We dance beneath the silver moon.
Together, we craft a symphony,
In this song, eternally free.

With every heartbeat, a refrain,
The song of us, a sweet domain.
In perfect harmony, we belong,
Together, forever, our love's song.

Echoes in a Quiet Room

In stillness, whispers softly play,
Memories linger, come what may.
Each shadow dances, softly seen,
In the quiet, where we've been.

The walls know tales we left behind,
Every sigh, a thought defined.
Moments captured in the air,
In this space, we find our care.

With every heartbeat, echoes chime,
Reminders of our precious time.
Silence speaks in gentle tones,
In this room, we're never alone.

The light filters through, warm and bright,
Illuminating love's pure light.
In every breath, a ghost of you,
In this quiet, our love rings true.

As the day fades into night,
Together still, our hearts take flight.
In the stillness, we've found a home,
In echoes, together, we roam.

Tides of Tenderness

Like waves that kiss the sandy shore,
Your love, a tide that I adore.
With every ebb, with every flow,
A gentle pull, a soft hello.

Beneath the stars, we drift and sway,
In the moonlight, we find our way.
With every whisper, every sigh,
Tides of tenderness draw nigh.

In the currents, we dance so free,
Two hearts blending in harmony.
As the ocean meets the sky,
In this love, we learn to fly.

Through stormy seas and gentle breeze,
Our hearts unite, our souls at ease.
In the dance of fate, we trust,
With every wave, our love is just.

As time flows on, we'll never part,
You're the anchor within my heart.
Together, we'll ride each wave,
In the tides of tenderness, we're brave.

Shadows of Affection

In the quiet of the night,
Shadows dance with delight,
Whispers soft, hearts align,
In these moments, love's sign.

Beneath the moon's gentle glow,
We find warmth in the flow,
Hands entwined, spirits soar,
Shadows linger, wanting more.

Shared secrets in the dark,
Every look ignites a spark,
Silent vows, eyes confess,
In shadows, we find bliss.

Every heartbeat, a story told,
In this warmth, never cold,
Wrapped in a tender embrace,
In shadows, we find grace.

Time stands still, as we sway,
Love alive in every way,
In the night, hearts react,
Shadows hold what we attract.

The Language of Fingers

Fingers brush in soft caress,
Speaking words that hearts confess,
In the silence, a soft dance,
Every touch, a whispered chance.

Tracing lines of fate and dream,
Every motion, a flowing stream,
Gently weaving tales of old,
In this language, love unfolds.

Like leaves swaying in the breeze,
Fingers speak with perfect ease,
Silent laughter in their play,
Words unspoken, hearts obey.

In the warmth of each embrace,
Fingers find their secret place,
Language rich without a sound,
In our touch, true love is found.

Through the night, a soft refrain,
Fingers dance, release the pain,
In this symphony so sweet,
Two souls meet, worlds complete.

Heartbeats in Harmony

In the rhythm of the night,
Two heartbeats, pure delight,
In sync beneath the stars,
Together, we heal our scars.

Every pulse, a gentle song,
In this dance, where we belong,
Breathing life, let love ignite,
In harmony, we take flight.

Through the chaos, calm remains,
Two heartbeats, breaking chains,
In the stillness, we are one,
Two hearts beating, life begun.

Every moment, sweetly shared,
In this bond, we are prepared,
For the trials life may bring,
In our hearts, we always sing.

Underneath the endless sky,
Together, we will fly high,
With each heartbeat, we will sway,
In harmony, love leads the way.

Silhouettes of Desire

In the dusk, shadows play,
Silhouettes dance, come what may,
Longing glances, sparks ignite,
In their forms, desire's light.

Each movement, a silent plea,
In the night, just you and me,
Like the stars, we intertwine,
In this dark, our hearts align.

Breathless whispers fill the air,
In this moment, we lay bare,
Silhouettes beneath the moon,
In this space, love's sweet tune.

With every glance, desire grows,
In the darkness, passion flows,
Two shadows merge, feeling free,
In this dance, just you and me.

As the night begins to fade,
In our hearts, the memories laid,
Silhouettes of what we crave,
In the morning, love will brave.

Shadows of a Shared Dream

In twilight's glow, whispers sigh,
As shadows dance, we draw nigh.
Fleeting hopes in whispered beams,
We chase the trails of shared dreams.

A echo lingers, softly spoken,
Each heartbeat ties, none are broken.
Through the veil of fading night,
Together, we embrace the light.

In moonlit paths, our secrets weave,
A tapestry only we perceive.
Steps in rhythm, hand in hand,
We stroll through hours so unplanned.

Beneath the stars, where wishes twirl,
In the stillness, our hearts unfurl.
Silent vows are gently cast,
In a dream, we're free at last.

These shadows hold a silent trust,
In every breath, we're one, we must.
Through night's embrace, our spirits soar,
With shared dreams, forevermore.

Beneath the Veil of Togetherness

In quiet moments, hearts align,
Beneath the veil, our souls entwine.
A gentle touch, a knowing glance,
In unity, we find our chance.

The world around us fades away,
As we create our own ballet.
With whispered thoughts and silent mirth,
We celebrate this sacred birth.

In laughter shared and burdens light,
We weave our way through day and night.
Through storms that come and shadows cast,
Together we will ever last.

Each breath a promise, softly made,
In every choice, our love displayed.
In every trial, we stand as one,
Beneath the stars, our journey's spun.

A fortress built on trust so deep,
In shared dreams, our spirits leap.
Within this veil, we find our home,
In togetherness, we freely roam.

Starlit Promises

Under skies where starlight plays,
We find our hopes in dazzling rays.
Each twinkle holds a sacred vow,
In the silence, we take a bow.

With every wish, our spirits rise,
Reflected in the night's soft sighs.
Promises dance in the soft light,
Whispered secrets take their flight.

As constellations map our fate,
We navigate through love's own gate.
In the cosmos, our dreams ignite,
Bathed in warmth, we shine so bright.

We gather stardust, hand in hand,
In this vast sea, our hearts will stand.
Together, we embrace the night,
With starlit promises shining bright.

So let us weave this cosmic thread,
With love and dreams as our steadfast bed.
In the heavens, forever roam,
With starlit promises, our home.

Threads of Connection

In every glance, a story weaves,
Connection grows as heart believes.
Through fragile strands, we are entwined,
A tapestry of souls combined.

In laughter shared, our colors blend,
With every moment, we transcend.
Threads of gold and silver shine,
In this design, your heart is mine.

The distance fades, our hearts align,
In whispered words, a soft divine.
From every struggle, strength is drawn,
In woven dreams, we'll carry on.

Each shared silence, a vow renewed,
With understanding, our spirits glued.
Together in this sacred dance,
Life's symphony, we'll take a chance.

Through every twist and every turn,
In this connection, we will learn.
So let us cherish every thread,
In this bond, our hearts are fed.

Illuminated Paths

Beneath the stars, we walk so free,
Each step a whisper, a gentle plea.
The moonlight guides our hopeful hearts,
In shadows deep, a new dawn starts.

The trees stand tall, their leaves a glow,
Reflecting dreams, in evening's flow.
With every breath, the night unfolds,
A tapestry of tales retold.

The river sings, its voice so clear,
In harmony, we draw it near.
With every current, time slips away,
As we embrace the night and day.

Paths entwined, our spirits soar,
Within this dance, we seek for more.
Together, we will find our way,
Illuminated by love's array.

Our journey bright, with every stride,
Eternal light, we will not hide.
For in this moment, hand in hand,
We create a world, our promised land.

The Essence of Together

In quiet strength, our hearts unite,
Two souls as one, a shared delight.
Through laughter's glow and sorrow's shade,
We weave the bonds that will not fade.

In fleeting moments, joy we find,
A sacred space, our hearts aligned.
With every challenge, love will grow,
A steadfast fire, a gentle glow.

The whispers soft, in evening's light,
Brush away worries, ease the night.
With every touch, a promise made,
In love's embrace, our fears allayed.

Through storms we sail, in calm we rest,
Together always, we are blessed.
For in this journey, hand in hand,
We write a tale, a perfect strand.

The essence pure, in unity,
A dance of hearts, twirling free.
In every heartbeat, ever near,
Together, love remains sincere.

Gossamer Threads of Affection

Like silken threads spun through the air,
Whispers of love, both soft and rare.
They weave our stories, tender and bright,
Glimmers of hope in the darkest night.

Fragile yet strong, they intertwine,
In every glance, a cherished sign.
With laughter's echo and gentle sighs,
These threads of warmth, a sweet surprise.

In every moment, we find our way,
Through tangled paths where shadows play.
Each heartbeat knits, with tender care,
A bond unspoken, a love laid bare.

As seasons change and time will flow,
These gossamer threads will gently grow.
For in their grasp, we stand as one,
With every dawn, a new day's sun.

They hold the stories of all we share,
In woven whispers that fill the air.
Though fragile, they carry deep affection,
Binding us close, a sweet connection.

Journey Through Love's Prism

Through love's prism, colors dance and sway,
A rainbow's kiss at the break of day.
Each hue a heartbeat, a moment shared,
A journey taken, a heart unscared.

In laughter's light, we find our way,
With each step forward, come what may.
The path is bright with every gleam,
A tapestry of love, a vivid dream.

Through trials faced and storms we've braved,
In each embrace, our spirits saved.
The spectrum glows with every tear,
In every shadow, love draws near.

With every glance, new shades emerge,
A swirling dance, an endless surge.
Together we paint the world anew,
With love's own brush, in every hue.

Our journey flows, a timeless art,
In every rhythm, we play our part.
Through love's prism, forever we'll see,
The beauty in you and the beauty in me.

Promises in the Breeze

Whispers dance through the trees,
Carried soft on the evening air.
Each promise floats with ease,
Caught in the twilight's gentle glare.

Moments pause, hearts entwined,
Underneath the painted skies.
In each sigh, love defined,
As stars begin to rise.

Dreams flutter like the leaves,
In colors bright and bold.
Together, our heart believes,
In stories waiting to be told.

The world fades, time is still,
Bound by trust, we find our way.
In the quiet, a shared thrill,
As night embraces the day.

Each breeze holds a secret tune,
Of laughter and soft refrain.
We dance under the moon,
As love calls us once again.

Cradle of Our Embrace

In the hush of twilight dim,
We find warmth in our retreat.
Soft shadows around us swim,
As our hearts begin to beat.

Fingers lace in sweet repose,
This cradle, a sacred space.
With every breath love glows,
In the echo of your grace.

Time slows down as we sway,
In the rhythm of gentle sighs.
Within this moment we stay,
Underneath the endless skies.

Whispers float, sweet serenade,
A melody crafted by fate.
In your arms, fears fade,
As we welcome love's own slate.

Together, we dare to dream,
Of horizons yet unseen.
In the dark, our hearts gleam,
With promises pure and keen.

Harmony of Two Souls

In the quiet, we align,
Two souls merging as one.
With every heartbeat, a sign,
Of a journey just begun.

Notes of laughter fill the air,
A symphony of delight.
In this space, beyond compare,
Where shadows give way to light.

Hands entwined, we find our tune,
A rhythm felt through our veins.
Underneath the watchful moon,
Love dances, unchained remains.

Each moment echoes with grace,
As stars twinkle in accord.
In our hearts, a sacred place,
Where we cherish love's reward.

Together, we craft the day,
With dreams woven side by side.
In harmony, come what may,
Our souls forever abide.

The Stillness of Us

In the stillness, we are found,
Two hearts beating as one sound.
Captured in a tender gaze,
Lost in love's unbroken maze.

Time slips softly through our hands,
As silence speaks without a word.
In this moment, life expands,
In the peace that we have stirred.

Whispers echo, soft and low,
Carried by the evening breeze.
In this space, our feelings grow,
As we move with perfect ease.

Here, worries drift away,
With every breath, the world fades.
In our hearts, love's sweet bouquet,
Blooms in vibrant, endless shades.

Together, stillness remains,
Where the universe aligns.
In the calm, our love sustains,
Forever in these quiet signs.

Echoes of Affection

In whispers soft, love's gentle sighs,
Under the moon, where our promise lies.
Hand in hand, we wander wide,
Each heartbeat like the ocean's tide.

Through fields of dreams, we tread with grace,
In laughter shared, we find our place.
The stars above, our guiding light,
In every shadow, our souls ignite.

Even as seasons change and fade,
In every moment, memories are laid.
Our echoes linger, a sweet refrain,
A melody woven, through joy and pain.

With each sunrise, love's colors bloom,
Painting our path, dispelling gloom.
In embrace so warm, we stand as one,
A story written, never to be done.

Whispers and laughter in the silent night,
With every heartbeat, our spirits take flight.
Together we dance, with fate's design,
In the echoes of affection, forever entwined.

The Heart's Canvas

Upon this canvas, colors blend,
Each brushstroke tells of love's sweet mend.
A palette rich with hopes and dreams,
In vibrant hues, life brightly gleams.

With every splash, a story flows,
Of whispered secrets, and tender throes.
The sun sets low, igniting the sky,
Artistry blooms, as feelings fly.

In chiaroscuro, shadows play,
Highlighting moments of joy and dismay.
With a gentle hand, we build and break,
Crafting a masterpiece, hearts awake.

Each stroke of fate, a reminder clear,
That love's creation is what we hold dear.
In collaboration, two souls combine,
On the heart's canvas, our lives intertwine.

As the final piece receives its frame,
We stand together, forever the same.
With every heartbeat, the colors thrive,
On the heart's canvas, our love's alive.

Silent Serenade of Devotion

In the hush of night, our hearts compose,
A silent tune that only love knows.
Notes of longing, softly played,
In the quiet, our vows are laid.

With gentle rhythms, souls intertwine,
In the stillness, your hand finds mine.
A melody sweet, on whispering air,
In the silence, we find what we share.

Through tender moments, we dance along,
Creating a symphony, pure and strong.
Each glance a note, each touch a chord,
In the silence of love, we are restored.

As the stars align, we hear love's song,
In the night, we know where we belong.
The serenade, a heartbeat's call,
In our devotion, we rise, we fall.

With every whisper that graces the night,
We embrace the melody, holding it tight.
In this serenade, forever we stay,
In the silence of love, we find our way.

In the Mirror of Souls

In the depths of eyes, reflections reside,
A journey of hearts where secrets abide.
Through the looking glass, we unveil,
A story of love, a timeless tale.

With every glance, a world ignites,
Where dreams converge in starry nights.
In the mirror of souls, we find our truth,
An eternal bond, the essence of youth.

As shadows dance, and light takes form,
In the silence, love's spirit is warm.
Our hearts echo, a symphonic hymn,
In the mirror's embrace, our spirits swim.

From laughter's glow to solemn sighs,
In reflections deep, our passion flies.
Together, we rise, through joy and pain,
In the mirror of souls, love shall reign.

For in every breath, your essence is near,
In the gaze we share, all doubts disappear.
In this sacred space, forever we dwell,
In the mirror of souls, love's story we tell.

Tides of Connection

Waves crash softly on the shore,
Echoes of laughter, hearts that soar.
Footprints linger in the sand,
A bond that time cannot disband.

In ebb and flow, we find our way,
Shared moments brightening the day.
Together we ride the ocean's crest,
In tides of trust, we are at our best.

As sunsets paint the sky anew,
Our dreams entwined, steadfast and true.
With every surge, our spirits rise,
Connected forever, under vast skies.

In whispers of the gentle breeze,
The world unveils its mysteries.
In every heartbeat, love does blend,
A circle drawn that knows no end.

By the shore where time stands still,
We gather strength, we find our will.
Hand in hand, come what may,
Together we'll brave each passing day.

The Palette of Us

Colors blend, a vibrant hue,
Each stroke tells stories, me and you.
In shades of laughter, tears, and joy,
We paint a map, girl and boy.

With every layer, we grow bold,
A canvas rich with tales untold.
In strokes of kindness, love ignites,
Painting dreams on endless nights.

Textures weave through heart and mind,
In tangled threads, our souls entwined.
With every splash, our spirits sing,
Creating beauty, life's shared fling.

Let colors swirl, let moments flow,
In this masterpiece, we glow.
Together, we craft, together, we trust,
In the palette of life, it's just us.

Each day a canvas, fresh and bright,
Together we bask in the light.
Through every shadow, we still shine,
In this artwork of love, divine.

Glimmers in the Dark

Stars twinkle softly, a night's embrace,
In the quiet, we find our place.
Flickering lights, whispers of hope,
Guiding our hearts, helping us cope.

In the shadows, we light the way,
Together we brave the darkest day.
With every spark, we rise anew,
In unison, our love shines through.

Moments flicker, like candle flame,
Each one cherished, never the same.
In the silence, our hearts align,
In glimmers shared, our spirits entwine.

Through storms and trials, we'll hold tight,
Finding comfort in love's pure light.
In every glance, there's strength to find,
A beacon shining, eternally blind.

Together we weave this tapestry,
Of dreams and wishes, you and me.
In the night's embrace, let's find our spark,
Creating magic, glimmers in the dark.

Resonance of Kindred Spirits

In the silence, our hearts converse,
Two souls dancing in the universe.
Each shared glance, a story begun,
In the warmth of friendship, we are one.

Echoes linger, a familiar tune,
Bright as the sun, soft as the moon.
In every laughter, in every tear,
We find a bond that draws us near.

Together we navigate life's sea,
Anchored in love, forever free.
With each heartbeat, we understand,
In kindred spirits, we take a stand.

Through storms we wander, hand in hand,
In unity, we make our stand.
With roots entwined beneath the ground,
In every silence, our love is found.

A symphony played with threads so fine,
Each note a heartbeat, yours and mine.
In this melody of souls aligned,
Forever grateful, our hearts intertwined.

In the Garden of Us

In the garden where we play,
Petals dance in soft array,
Whispers float on gentle breeze,
Blooming love among the trees.

Sunlight kisses every flower,
Every moment, our shared hour,
Roots entwined beneath the ground,
In this space, our hearts are found.

Colors bright, both bold and sweet,
In each pathway, our hearts meet,
Butterflies in joyful flight,
Guided by the soft moonlight.

Through the seasons, hand in hand,
In this haven, love will stand,
Harvest dreams that freely grow,
In the garden, love will flow.

Every raindrop sings a tune,
Underneath the watchful moon,
With each bloom, we find our way,
In the garden, we will stay.

Serenading the Stars

Beneath the vast and starry sky,
We share our dreams, just you and I,
Every twinkle tells a tale,
Of love that will forever sail.

Gentle breezes bring a song,
In this night where we belong,
The moonlight dances on your face,
In your arms, I find my place.

Constellations whisper softly,
Guiding hearts toward destiny,
Weaving wishes, bold and bright,
Serenading through the night.

Galaxies spin in endless flow,
As starlight sets our spirits aglow,
Hand in hand, we'll find our way,
Through the night and into day.

Each note played on cosmic strings,
Echoes of our love that rings,
In the silence, hear the roar,
Serenading forevermore.

Calming Waves of Affection

Upon the shore, where waters meet,
The sound of love is soft and sweet,
Waves unfold in gentle grace,
Each ebb, a warm embrace.

Footprints marking the sandy land,
Together, we will always stand,
As the tide rolls in and out,
In this love, we have no doubt.

The horizon stretches far and wide,
In the waves, our hearts confide,
Every splash, a story shared,
In this moment, we are spared.

Seagulls call, an echoing sound,
In this haven, bliss is found,
With every tide and sunset's hue,
Calming waves that speak of you.

Let the ocean's rhythm play,
Guiding us along the way,
In this dance of waves, let's stay,
Calming love, come what may.

Embracing Silence

In the quiet, love resounds,
In the hush, our truth is found,
Words unspoken, yet so clear,
In this stillness, you are here.

Gentle breaths, a soft refrain,
In the silence, joy alleviates pain,
Holding hands, our hearts align,
In the peace, our souls entwine.

Morning light breaks, soft and true,
In the silence, it's me and you,
Each heartbeat, a silent call,
In our world, we have it all.

Moments linger, sweetly spun,
In this space, two hearts are one,
Every glance, our love ignites,
In the quiet, stars take flight.

As the evening gently sighs,
In the silence, love still tries,
Embracing all that we believe,
In each heartbeat, we perceive.

A Symphony of Bonds

In whispers soft, our hearts entwine,
Each note we play, in perfect time.
Together we rise, through storm and sun,
A harmony found, two souls as one.

With every laugh, a melody sweet,
In silent glances, our rhythms meet.
With every step, a dance we weave,
In this symphony, we both believe.

The world may change, but here we stand,
Creating music, hand in hand.
When darkness falls, our light will glow,
In the symphony of love, we'll grow.

Through trials faced, our song stays bright,
A tether strong, a guiding light.
In every chord, we find our place,
In this sweet dance, we embrace.

Together forged, through thick and thin,
In life's grand tune, we always win.
Our symphony will reign, never cease,
In bonds of love, we find our peace.

The Art of Togetherness

In quiet moments, side by side,
We paint our dreams, with hearts so wide.
With every smile, we brush the sky,
In strokes of joy, we learn to fly.

Through tangled paths, our fingers trace,
The beauty found in every space.
With laughter shared, we build our home,
In the art of love, we're never alone.

In gentle whispers, secrets flow,
With every tear, together we grow.
Through storms and sun, we craft our tale,
In unity strong, we'll never pale.

The colors blend, in shades of trust,
Creating beauty, as all dreams must.
In every stroke, we find our way,
A masterpiece, come what may.

And when the world fades out of sight,
Our hearts will shine, a guiding light.
In the art of togetherness, we'll be,
A canvas bright, for all to see.

Chasing Sunbeams

With open arms, we greet the day,
Beneath the skies, we laugh and play.
Our feet embrace the golden ground,
As sunbeams dance all around.

In fields of joy, we run and twirl,
As vibrant colors start to whirl.
With every ray, our spirits soar,
Chasing dreams, forevermore.

Through summer's breath, and winter's chill,
We find the warmth in love's sweet thrill.
As shadows lengthen, we'll not despair,
For sunbeams shine in every prayer.

With hearts ablaze, we'll find our way,
In each soft glow, we dare to stay.
For in this chase, we've come to know,
The light of love will always grow.

So let us dance, and let us gleam,
Forever bound, in this bright dream.
Chasing sunbeams, hand in hand,
In love's embrace, together we'll stand.

The Softness Between Us

In tender moments, silence speaks,
A quiet bond, a love that peaks.
With every touch, the world fades out,
In the softness, we hear no doubt.

Our hearts entwined, like vines so strong,
In each other's arms, where we belong.
With gentle sighs, the night unfolds,
In warmth and whispers, love beholds.

Through peaceful nights and sunny days,
In the simplest things, our hearts ablaze.
With every glance, our spirits meet,
In the softness, life feels complete.

As shadows loom, we'll brave the storm,
With tender strength, we find our form.
In every challenge, we rise anew,
For in the softness, I find you.

So let us linger, in this embrace,
With hearts aligned, we leave a trace.
In the softness between us, we find,
A sacred love, forever intertwined.

Milton Keynes UK
Ingram Content Group UK Ltd.
UKHW021824311024
450535UK00010B/200